This Book Belongs To:

_____

TEST YOUR PENS
 AND
PENCILS HERE

FIREFIGHTER

Doctor

FILM DIRECTOR

Chef

ELECTRICIAN

Police
Officer

Ship
Captain

Dentist

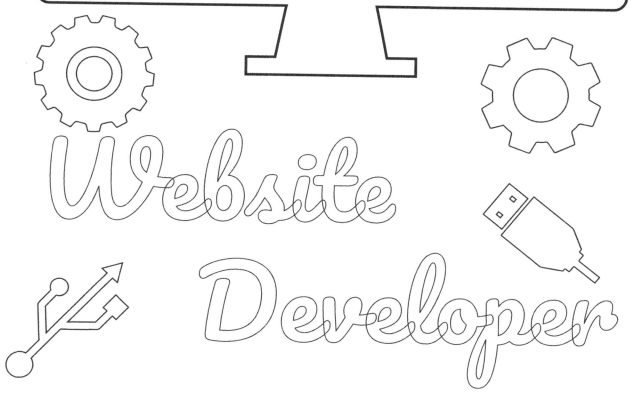

Website Developer

Construction Worker

Karate Instructor

abracadabra

Magician

Stay Curious little one

GRADUATE TO PROFESSOR

ARTIFICIAL INTELLIGENCE ENGINEER

Made in the USA
Las Vegas, NV
09 May 2023

71828468R00031